PU

Dedication

To all the dogs who ever were
and those who are to be,
we dedicate this newly book
called Puppy A B C

About this Book…

To the young dog, or puppy, who desires to improve his or her understanding of language, we dedicate this book.

You are about to take a journey of words which we hope will enrich your life as well as your vocabulary.

While every word you need to know in a lifetime is not represented, many words you need to know pretty darn quick are herein included.

Each word is clearly defined, and most are provided with examples of usage.

Furthermore, each page is complemented by a blank page for you, or a friend, to illustrate yourself.

In this way, you will enliven this first dictionary with your own personality.

PUPPY A-B-C

A Puppy's First Dictionary
- or -
A Dictionary for Young Dogs

A

Always   as in *hungry:* Puppies are *always* hungry

B

Bad   what People think you are when you do any of the following: [see Bite, Chew, Dig]

Ball   a small, round object with many dent marks; [see Teeth]

Bark — your natural sound, to be used as the mood strikes

Bath — unless you are considered a *water dog*, this humiliating experience is to be avoided at all costs; however, if you must have one, try not to let other dogs see it happen

Bed — 1. as in *dog bed*: your assigned place to sleep; 2. a more comfortable place to sleep used by People and on which you may not

Beg — what People think you're doing when all you really want is Something to Eat!

Biscuit — a small, crisp food item of which one is never enough

Bite	your natural tendency to grab things with your teeth [see Bad]
Bone	a small, hard object on which to practice biting and chewing techniques; sometimes tasty, and even more so after being buried for a while

C

Chase	your natural ability to go after and grab things; [see Tail]
Chew	your natural ability to use your teeth to best advantage, often misunderstood by others [see Don't]
Collar	a diabolically clever device which is fastened around your neck and on which various charms are hung; not pleasant, but the charms are often cute.

Come	a command word used by People which you may usually ignore as it is of little significance
Command	a word or group of terms that People seem to think will allow them to control, motivate or in other ways direct your natural behavior; you may ignore for the most part; however, the command word *Sit* may be complied with on occasion as it has been known to produce Biscuit or Cookie
Cookie	a small, crisp food item of which one is never enough
Couch	a largish, comfortable piece of furniture on which you are probably not allowed, except when no one is looking [see Off]

Crate   a wire cage said by People to be cozy and den-like for you, but by which you are not fooled one little bit

Cute   another word for you, most often used during your first six months, thereafter only on occasion

D

Dad   a type of People with whom you may share quarters, subject to your approval; often considered the Boss; [also see Couch and Zzzz]

Dig   your natural urge to unearth earth, often misunderstood by People [see Don't]

Dinner   a type of meal served; typically inadequate and boring

Dish	the container in which Dinner is served and usually more attractive
Doggie	another word for you, sometimes combined with Bad or Good, occasionally with Cute, most often used during your first six months, with instances of Bad far outnumbering the latter two terms
Don't	a command word that indicates the speaker doesn't understand the importance of what you are doing
Door	the way out, or in some cases, the way in, or in some cases either, or both
Down	a command word that indicates the speaker doesn't understand that you need to be up

E

Eat   one of two or three main things
that you are meant to do in this life

F

Family   generally, those with whom you
choose to share; may include
People or higher order beings such
as yourself

Fetch   a command word that indicates the
speaker has misplaced some item of
obvious insignificance; an
obsessive-compulsive disorder in
some People

Food   anything you can fit into your
mouth, bite, chew and swallow, with
variations in nutritive value, taste
and texture

Frisbee   a flat, round object thrown towards you in short, repeated intervals by People for inordinate lengths of time; the only way to stop this madness is to chew the Frisbee to bits, thereby rendering it useless

G

Go   another of three or four main things that you are meant to do in this life

Good   another name for You, but sadly overlooked in many circumstances

Grrr   your natural warning sound to be used as the mood strikes; it is not necessary that any real threat be present – imaginary ones are acceptable

H

Home   1. where you and your People reside; 2. where you are directed by

Others when they do not
understand you have Places to Go

House   a structure in which you and your
           Family reside; (not to be confused
           with the defamatory term "dog
           house" which has nothing to do
           with you)

I

In   what you want when you are Out
           [see Out]

J

Jump   your natural method of greeting
           People, often misunderstood;
           similar, but far superior to the more
           awkward People handshake [see
           Down]

K

Kibble   a type of food item often served as Dinner in your Dish; typically unappetizing, boring and of questionable nutritive value, but to which you may resort in times of extreme need

L

Lap   what appears when People sit; (not to be confused with the command word Sit which, when complied with, produces the appropriate and correct posture)

Leash   sometimes called a *lead*, this long strap is attached to the collar [see Collar] and used by People to try to keep you under control; moderately successful; not too odious if used for walks [see Walk]

Lick   your natural inclination to run your tongue over, and occasionally into,

various surfaces or orifices, some of which may be considered off-limits by People, although they consider others perfectly acceptable; it is often hard to determine which is which

Love   an emotion which you naturally give unstintingly to People, but which they return only as the mood strikes, or when they want something from you

M

Mean   as in *"I mean it!"* [see Now]; this expression is usually directed at you when some natural behavior of yours has confused your People

Mess   as in *"Who made this mess?"* [see Bad; also Mean]

Mom	a type of People with whom you may share quarters [see Dad], and who is *really* the Boss

N

No	a command word that indicates the speaker disagrees fundamentally with what you are doing or are thinking of doing or are about to do
No No	another command word that indicates the speaker has a possible speech impediment or stutters
Now	an adjunct word occasionally used with other command words [see Don't, Down, Off] that indicates the speaker lacks patience

O

Off	a command word that indicates the speaker doesn't understand you need to be *on*

Oh no   [see No and No No] a variation of
               those command words indicating
               the speaker is at a low ebb or
               perhaps the end of his or her rope;
               an actual rope need not be present,
               however

Ouch   [see Bite, Chew, Teeth] a term
               expressed by People indicating they
               have an extremely low level of pain
               tolerance; ignore

Out   what you want when you are in [see
               In]; also, when used with force, a
               command word indicating the
               speaker may be at the Oh no stage

P

Pee   your natural function to release
               excess liquid, useful in labeling
               various objects of personal property
               [see Out and X]

People	one or more of the two-legged variety; also the Lower Orders; those whom you learn to tolerate and, superficially, obey when to your advantage
Play	another of four or five main things you are meant to do in this life
Poop	your natural function to liberate unusable Food of every kind except liquids [see Pee]; also that of other Higher Order beings like yourself which identifies what kind of Food, among other things, they have eaten recently; normally an outdoor activity, but if In, see Out and Now
Puppy	another word for you, most often heard in your first 6 to 12 months of life; usually in combination with Cute, occasionally heard with Good, more likely with Bad

Q

Quit   as in *"Quit that!"* [see Off, Down], a
term indicating the speaker doesn't
understand, for example, you need
to be On, or Up; in more serious
cases, may further indicate the
speaker is nearing the Oh No stage

R

Ready?   a term with a rising inflection
directed at you by the speaker,
usually accompanied by raised
eyebrows and occasionally a smiley
face; you may respond favorably to
this term as it has been known to
produce Play, Ride, and Go
behavior in People

Ride   an activity with People usually
involving a moving vehicle, often
resulting in Play and generally
thought to be fun – with one or
two important exceptions [see Vet,
also Upchuck]

Run	another of five or six main things you are meant to do in this life

S

Sit	a command word with which you may generally comply [see Lap] producing only momentary sensations of obedience which soon disappear, especially if immediately followed by Cookie or Biscuit
Stay	a command word originating from Sit, yet far more onerous; [for advanced puppies only]; compliance produces prolonged feelings of obedience and should at all costs be avoided

T

Table	a tallish piece of furniture off of which People periodically consume Food; generally forbidden to you, but may be approached if you assume the guise of Cute Puppy

Tail	when present, the farthest part of you from your teeth; as the mood strikes it may be wagged (if present); also [see Chase]
Teeth	your natural biting and chewing instruments, applied, for example, to Food, Biscuit, Cookie, and occasionally People; [see Ouch]
Toy	any item in your possession at the moment; may be bitten, chewed, eaten, or fetched as the mood strikes; you may consider texture and taste, but not necessarily nutritive value
Treat	any food item over and above the minimum required; may appear as Cookie, Biscuit, Chew Stick, or Food stolen from People or another dog

U

Up	what you want when you are Down [see Lap]

Upchuck	your normal reaction to Food or other item that turns out to be unacceptable; also what may happen during Ride

V

Vet	one who cannot be trusted generally, e.g. will present Cookie or Biscuit concurrently with needle or thermometer [see Ouch, or don't see]; on occasion, turns out to be tolerable

W

Wag	your natural tail function [if tail present]; used to display various moods, usually one of happiness or readiness to play; occasionally employed to indicate "I didn't do that."
Wait	a command word that indicates your People have forgotten something

Walk	an outdoor activity sometimes accompanied by the leash [see Leash] often used to encourage bodily functions [see Poop and Pee] and which can, if you are lucky, result in play [see Play]
Who	a word used by People which may refer to you occasionally, as in *"Who did this?"* [see No No]; the sound of this word may be particularly loud when directed at you

X

X	as in *"marks the spot"*; as you mature, you will fully grasp the finer nuances of this concept

Y

You	when used by People, this word may often be irritable-sounding, shrill and/or loud [see Mess and Who]

Z

Zzzz   a sound often produced by Dad [see
            Couch]; this sound invites you to
            jump up, wag, chew, bark and in
            general indicates that it is time to
            play

We hope you enjoyed *Puppy A-B-C* and that you
provided lots of colorful illustrations.

Have fun with your puppy or young dog and notice
how many words he or she learns.

My dog Jake knows lots of words, including many in
this book as well as others I think he made up
himself.

Jake is an old dog now, but he learned words right
away when he was a puppy. I was amazed!

You can write Jake and me at

2mungers@gmail.com

bye for now!

Made in the USA
Columbia, SC
18 December 2017